GW01398505

Original title:
A Feast of Thankful Hearts

Author: Natalia Harrington
ISBN HARDBACK: 978-9916-94-360-1
ISBN PAPERBACK: 978-9916-94-361-8

Porchlight Gatherings

Under the glow of the big porch light,
We all munch on leftovers from last night.
The pie that's so lumpy, and frankly a wreck,
Our stomachs are full, but we're still a wreck.

Grandpa's telling jokes that never land right,
We laugh so hard; it's pure delight.
Cousins are bickering over who can dance,
While Auntie pretends she still has a chance.

Reflections on Unity

We gather 'round with faces aglow,
Fighting for space in the last taco show.
Who's hogging the guac? Let's point out the truth,
We've come for the feast, and the shenanigans, too.

A toast to the moments that make us all cheer,
To chaos and laughter, and far too much beer.
In this wild mix, we find our good cheer,
A family of nutters, year after year.

The Warmth of Companionship

Around the table, food piled so high,
We shove in the turkey, oh my, oh my!
Each bite's a battle, a tasty delight,
With gravy that stains the shirt worn so tight.

We share silly stories, and laughter's our guide,
Who's stealing the biscuits? Let's set aside pride!
With food coma creeping, we still joke and beam,
Together we're perfectly unhinged, it seems.

Harvesting Joy

Crunching on carrots that taste like a dream,
While chatting about who won last week's scheme.
The salad's a rainbow, not quite a delight,
But the punch is a hit—oh, what a bright light!

As pie fills the air, it's a sugary haze,
The kitchen's a circus of wild, funny ways.
With hearts full and messy, we hold hands and cheer,
Here's to the gatherings, we love them all year!

Elements of the Heart

In pots of soup, we lose our spoons,
Our shoes are stuck to sticky floors.
Laughter hides behind the tunes,
While grandma fights the kitchen chores.

Mashed potatoes flying high,
Dancing around the turkey's fate.
Like clouds that chase a sunny sky,
We take our seats and hope for fate.

Kindred Spirits at the Table

At the table piled with pies,
Uncles claim they've lost their name.
Aunties gossip, roll their eyes,
While kids delight in food and games.

A cousin's laugh is like a song,
As we toast with glasses clinked.
But who stole grandma's cake? So wrong!
Oh wait, it's me—I'm now distinct!

Laughter and Love Served

From broccoli to cake so sweet,
We dish out jokes like butter spread.
And if you don't like what you eat,
Just bury it beneath the bread!

The dog waits 'neath the table's end,
His eyes like saucers, full of dreams.
While we all laugh and love, my friend,
He snags the scraps, or so it seems.

Reveling in the Riches of Togetherness

With dishes stacked as high as pride,
We dive in deep, no time to waste.
A pie debates, 'Should I hide?'
While forks and laughter intermixed taste.

And as we munch through bites galore,
The stories spill like mashed up bread.
We laugh until we're tired, sore,
Next year, more pies! We'll feast instead.

The Light of Gratitude

In the kitchen, clinks and clatters,
A turkey's dancing, oh, how it matters!
The stuffing's bubbling, then it flips,
All that prep work, can't wait for the sips!

Grandma's secret sauce is a little too bold,
Uncle Joe's tales, they never get old.
With every laugh and overcooked pie,
We roll our eyes, then we give it a try!

Cousins are plotting their next big prank,
While dodging the sprouts, thanks to our rank.
Sweet potatoes glisten like jewels on a screen,
But where's that chocolate cake? It's fit for a queen!

So here's to the joy, the mess and the cheer,
Raising our glasses of fizzy root beer.
In this wild chaos, we find our delight,
With hearts full of laughter, it all feels just right!

Community at the Table

Gathered close, plates piled high,
Mashed potatoes flying, oh my, oh my!
A side of laughter, served fresh and warm,
With a dash of chaos, it's our perfect charm!

Aunt Lucy's dancing, last year's big hit,
While Grandpa snoozes, not a care, not a bit.
The dog's on the table, claiming his space,
As we try to save that last slice of grace!

The kids are debating on who's best at chess,
Dad just wants silence, he's feeling the stress.
Forgotten the dishes, oh, what a scene,
It's dessert time now, it's all about cream!

So cheers to the moments, both silly and bright,
Through laughter and food, we're all feeling right.
In this wonderful circus, we're grateful and free,
With love served on plates, oh, what glee!

Whispered Wishes

In the kitchen, pots collide,
A spoon that danced, a fork that pried.
Mashed potatoes flying high,
Oh my, a turkey's about to cry!

Pumpkin pie takes a wild spin,
With whipped cream splatters, let the fun begin!
Family chuckles fill the air,
Who knew cooking could be this rare?

A Tapestry of Togetherness

Gathered round the table wide,
Napkin hats that kids abide.
The dog sneaks treats from the floor,
While Grandpa snores on the door!

Uncle Bob shares jokes with flair,
But Cousin Sue just pulls her hair.
Through it all, our laughter blends,
A quirky tribe that never bends.

Cherished Traditions

Grandma's recipe, a family tease,
Who forgot to say, 'Don't set it, please!'
Cookies burned, we start to cry,
Then someone shouts, 'Let's make a pie!'

Silly games replace the fuss,
In every chaos, we find the plus.
With goofy smiles and chatter loud,
Our joyous hearts form one proud crowd.

Resilience and Kindness

The table wobbles, the soup does spill,
Sister's giggles we can't distill.
A toast with juice, oh what a sight,
"Cheers to our messes, and all that's right!"

With spills and thrills and stories told,
Traditions wrap us like a mold.
Through ups and downs, we stand in line,
Kindness makes the whole meal divine.

Echoing Laughter

In the kitchen, pots go clang,
A turkey's dance, the oven sang.
Mashed potatoes start to fly,
As gravy rivers wave goodbye.

Uncle Joe spills the cranberry,
The dog sneaks in, oh so merry!
A pie on his snout, what a sight,
We all laugh till the clock strikes night.

Threads of Joy

Grandma knits with twinkling eyes,
With yarn more colorful than the skies.
Plates are piled with too much food,
But Mom's still worried, oh so crude!

Cousins wrestle on the floor,
While Aunt Sue checks the pantry door.
"More snacks!" she hollers, "Quickly, please!"
As we all giggle, with hearts at ease.

Abundant Blessings

The salad's tossed with love and cheer,
But the dressing lands right near my ear.
With every bite, we share a jest,
Who knew a fork could be so blessed?

Dealing with a rogue bread roll,
That just decided to take a stroll.
We chase it 'round the dining room,
Laughter bursting, chasing gloom.

Kinship and Kindness

As stories swirl like autumn leaves,
We toast to joy and share our eves.
With each joke, the spirits soar,
We giggle, guffaw, and want more!

Seated close, our hearts unite,
Even the cat joins this delight.
Through blunders, laughter finds its way,
In this warm, shared, silly display.

Heartfelt Conviviality

Gather 'round the table, dear,
With dishes piled up high,
Uncle Joe has dropped his slice,
Now the cat is starting to fly!

Laughter spills like gravy,
A turkey's tango on display,
Aunt Sue's pie took flight last night,
Oh, how we wish it would stay!

Slices of Gratitude

Pass the rolls, but watch your grip,
They've got butter, and they've got zip!
With every bite, we clear our throats,
To thank the cook for all the oats!

Watch the kids with pie on faces,
Competing for the sweetest spaces,
While Grandpa shows his dancing skills,
We celebrate with hearty thrills.

Harmony in Diversity

Here's a salad, dressed with cheer,
And grandma's recipe, oh dear!
Spicy, sweet, and quite a mix,
This spread's a wild culinary fix!

With every culture on a plate,
We blend our flavors, it's first-rate,
A dash of laughter, a sprinkle of spice,
Together we feast, so very nice!

Thankfulness in Every Bite

Mashed potatoes like fluffy clouds,
With gravy rivers, oh, so proud,
We cheer for veggies, too, you see,
Their funny faces full of glee!

Thankful for the quirky ways,
That family comes to swap their flays,
With every bite, we share a grin,
For joy is where the love begins!

Whispers of Thankfulness

In the kitchen, chaos reigns,
Turkey's in the oven, we're losing our brains.
Grandma's gravy, a secret delight,
Sneaky cousin steals pie, what a sight!

Laughter fills the air, it's loud and bright,
Uncle Joe's jokes? They don't quite hit right.
Sisters drop rolls, and oh what a mess,
But we can't help but love the happiness!

Bountiful Dreams

Plates overflowing, like a mountain so high,
A voting war over the last pumpkin pie.
Tummies are rumbling, we let out a cheer,
'If you touch my dessert, you're banned from next year!'

Cousins and kids all play hide and seek,
Peeled potatoes? We say, 'Not this week!'
The dog steals a drumstick, claims his own throne,
Looks like leftovers might be a bit blown!

Gathering Around the Table

Around the table, the stories unfold,
Aunt Mildred's tacos, a legend retold.
With forks held high, we declare our fate,
Sweet potato casserole? Just don't wait!

The cat, oh my, is eyeing that pie,
One swift leap, and the dessert will fly.
Napkins are tossed, a food fight breaks free,
But love is the real feast, that's clearly the key!

Echoes of Appreciation

Echoes of laughter bounce off the wall,
As Dad tries his best not to drop his fall.
Sisters giggling, holding their sides,
Who's the best cook? Well, that's where it hides!

The plates stack high, like a tower of fun,
Someone's foot lands where the sweet rolls run.
Thankful for moments that make us all laugh,
With smiles as big as the turkey's fat calf!

Moments to Savor

When the pie is devoured, who stole the last slice?
A turkey named Fred thinks he's quite nice.
With gravy like glue, he sticks to the plate,
And Aunt Lucy's hat? Oh, it's quite the fate!

The toast for the meal, oh such a delight,
But Uncle Joe's jokes just don't seem quite right.
As we laugh and we munch, the mishaps unfold,
Like Grandma's surprise—a new hip made of gold!

Each moment we share is wrapped up in cheer,
While the dog plots to steal every roll that's near.
With laughter and love, our hearts really soar,
As we gobble and grin, asking, 'Can we have more?'

Thankfulness Under the Stars

Beneath twinkling lights, we gather around,
But who brought the dog that just won't sit down?
With marshmallows flying, a sticky sweet fight,
And Aunt Sue's loud singing—what a delight!

The stars wink with joy at our silly charade,
While Uncle Bob swears he made the best grade.
With pies stacked so high, we all take a peek,
Yet somehow they vanish by the end of the week.

As we clink our glasses and giggle a ton,
Who borrowed my shoes? Oh wait, that was fun!
With joy in our hearts, and grand tales to spin,
Under stars, we remind ourselves where to begin.

Gratitude in the Air

The scent of cooked stuffing dances with glee,
While Cousin Ed dreams of his own pumpkin spree.
With a wink and a laugh, my dog sneaks a bite,
And we lock eyes and know—what a humorous sight!

At the table we gather, with jokes on the side,
And Grandma's old stories, oh how we abide!
The food's piled up high, like a turkey tower,
Yet somehow we always seem to lose track of power.

With forks at the ready, we nibble and munch,
While trying to find a polite way to crunch.
As laughter erupts, the spirit ignites,
Thankfulness blooms in our quirky delights.

Harvest Moon Blessings

As the moon paints the night with a silver white glow,
We gather to feast, but there's chaos in tow.
The corn on the cob plays musical chairs,
While Kevin complains that this chair's for his airs!

With pumpkins and laughter, we fill to the brim,
As Aunt Poppy's loud snoring interrupts the hymn.
The blessings are many, the stories run wide,
Yet the truth is clear—what a hilarious ride!

With every rich morsel, we raise up a cheer,
For moments of joy that we hold so dear.
As the harvest moon beams and our hearts are all stirred,
We count our good fortunes in laughs, not in words.

Blessings on the Wind

A turkey trotted 'round the room,
His waddle danced away the gloom.
The mashed potatoes held a grin,
As gravy poured out like a win.

The pumpkin pie looked quite divine,
Whipped cream swirled like a fine design.
Yet cousin Joe brought fruitcake bold,
We laughed as he said, "It's worth its weight in gold!"

Uncle Bob wore a goofy hat,
He said, "I'm here to taste and chat!"
The cranberry sauce made a mess,
But just you wait, it's all a guess!

So raise your glass, here's a toast,
To food and fun we love the most!
With laughter ringing in the air,
Let's dine 'til we cannot bear!

Gathering in Harmony

The kids all bounced in joyful cheer,
While Aunt Sue hid behind a deer.
The dog snagged a roll, oh dear me!
We laughed and cried 'til we could see.

Grandma brought out her secret stew,
With mystery ingredients, who knew?
"I made it with love," she said with pride,
As Uncle Jim sat wide-eyed side.

With forks raised high in silly fight,
Who got the biggest piece tonight?
As everyone claimed they should win,
The pies rolled in, let the feasting begin!

A chorus of voices, a big cheer,
In harmony, we hold each dear.
With every bite and every smile,
We gather 'round for quite a while!

The Flavor of Gratitude

Sweet potato likes to play it cool,
While green beans join the dinner pool.
Cornbread's jumping, full of zest,
It knows that it's the very best!

The stuffing's dancing on the plate,
"Don't rush me now, don't tempt your fate!"
While salad sings with leafy flair,
"Don't dress me down, I'm loved with care!"

We pass the rolls like secret spies,
While laughter bubbles, oh, how it flies!
And just when we think we're done,
More dishes come—oh, what a run!

So let's dig in, enjoy the ride,
With every flavor, joy inside.
The meal's like magic, in every bite,
Gratitude sparkles like stars at night!

Heartstrings and Harvests

A table spread with smiles so wide,
Each dish a joy we cannot hide.
John's jokes land like sweet syrup thick,
While Aunt May's dance is quite the trick!

The apples danced in cider pools,
As cousins played a game of fools.
With heartstrings pulled from every plate,
We feast and laugh—it's truly fate!

Turkey made a grand old scene,
As Grandma unveiled her secret bean.
We cheered with forks, what fun we share,
In every dish, love's sprinkled everywhere!

So here's to us, to joy and cheer,
To love that blooms when we are near.
With heartstrings joined, let's celebrate,
This harvest time, oh, isn't it great!

Remembrance in Every Flavor

In a pot, we toss our dreams,
A dash of laughter, it seems.
Grandpa's socks, a funny sight,
While Aunt Edna whips up a bite.

We pine for turkey, brave and bold,
Yet Uncle Joe sells stories old.
With pumpkin pie and spuds that dance,
We find ourselves in quite a trance.

The table's set, so grand, so wide,
With mismatched chairs, we take our stride.
Each shared glance sparks a witty tale,
As cousin Timmy starts to wail.

So raise a glass of fizzy cheer,
To friendships that are always near.
In every morsel, tales unfold,
And hearts are warmed by love untold.

Warm Embrace of Family

Gathered round, a lively crew,
With grinning faces, how 'bout you?
Auntie's casserole, too much cheese,
We tease her gently, 'Please, oh please!'

Silly hats and laughter loud,
Dancing kids, an awkward crowd.
With every mishap, joy does swell,
As Grandpa drops the Jell-O, well!

A toast to kin, with drinks raised high,
Though some spill wine, they don't know why.
In every hug, a giggle's found,
As love wraps tight, like blankets round.

So here's to moments, bright and sweet,
With every mishap, life's a treat.
In the warm embrace, we find our place,
Amongst the laughter, we all embrace.

The Taste of Together

With every bite, a smile returns,
As grandma's gravy spirals and churns.
A roll falls flat, we cannot stop,
As cousin Jake does a table hop.

With spoons a-clanging and glasses cheers,
We share our lives, our hopes, our fears.
Each dish a joke, each laugh a gift,
As family bonds begin to lift.

From mashed potatoes to pecan pie,
A taste for every unique vibe.
In every nibble, a joyful spree,
Where calories vanish, only glee!

So eat and laugh, don't hold back,
For every crumb leads to a new track.
Together we feast, we sing, we shout,
For love is what this day's about.

Gathering of Souls

Outfits gleam, a colorful sight,
As Uncle Lou takes off in flight.
His turkey dance makes everyone grin,
While grandma's pie fights back again!

We gather close, this lively bunch,
With stories old, we love to munch.
The dog sneaks in for a dropped bite,
While aunties fuss and tease outright.

In this delightful, bustling scene,
We find connections tied like string.
With playful jabs and laughter great,
We feast together, it's never late.

So cheers to mishaps, cheers to cheer!
A gathering of souls we hold dear.
In every smile, a spark will ignite,
As we share our joy in the soft twilight.

Cherished Company

Gathered 'round the table, we cheer,
With mashed potatoes and jokes we hold dear.
Uncle Joe's stories, a twist or a lie,
Gravy spills everywhere, oh me, oh my!

Sister's pie, a sight to behold,
With so much whipped cream, it's daring and bold.
Cousin's dance moves, a flailing delight,
We laugh till it hurts, what a glorious night!

Each clink of the glasses, a toast with a grin,
To mishaps and laughter, let the fun begin!
Mom's secret recipe, that nobody knows,
Is it really just pizza? Who ever knows?

With love, we create this grand joy-filled scene,
As we fight for dessert, like a movie on screen.
Thankful for laughter, and friends full of cheer,
In this comedy of life, we hold dear.

Reflections in a Cornucopia

A cornucopia spills over, what a sight,
Vegetables chatting, in colors so bright.
The carrots are gossiping, peas join the fun,
While silly old potatoes pretend they can run!

Pumpkins are chuckling, they just can't stop,
As cranberries tumble and hop, hop, hop.
Cabbage and lettuce, they twirl in a dance,
And all of the veggies are lost in a trance.

The fruit bowl is laughing, a jolly old tune,
Berries are bouncing beneath the full moon.
Apples debate who has the best shine,
While bananas slip up in a comedic line!

We gather together, a flavorsome mess,
With jokes about salads that truly impress.
In this playful garden, we share hearty cheer,
Grateful for laughter, our favorite time of year.

Toasts to the Tapestry of Life

Raise your glass high, with chips on the side,
Each toast a wild tale we cannot confide.
Grandpa's adventures, like legends of yore,
Thumping the table, as everyone roars!

Sister's at it again with her jokes about cats,
While brother keeps saying, "Let's talk about bats!"
A tapestry woven of laughter and tears,
Mom rolls her eyes at our mischief through years.

With cheers for all moments, both messy and grand,
We celebrate life as we nail down our plan.
For the pudding is jiggly and wobbles in glee,
As we toast to the chaos of being so free!

Endless rounds of laughter, like bubbles that pop,
We cherish these quirks, they never will stop.
With each silly moment, our bond grows more tight,
In the warmth of the gathering, everything's right.

Luminaries of Gratitude

Under the moonlight, we share our delight,
With twinkling laughter that dances so bright.
A jester's performance, pure magic to see,
As Uncle Frank juggles, spilling his tea!

Giggles erupt when the cat makes a leap,
Plopping right down on the pile, in a heap.
Our stories unite us, mix laughter with love,
Thankful for family, sent from above.

With candles a-glow, our shadows take flight,
Painting the walls with our shared silly night.
For we gather together, each quirk in our heart,
Grateful for moments that won't drift apart.

So here's to the humor, the love, and the play,
In this banquet of joy, we all find our way.
With laughter as lifeblood, a tapestry spun,
We shine in this gathering, our hearts all as one.

Nourishing Connections

Gather 'round the table, cheers!
Pass the pies and laugh at fears.
Uncle Joe drops his turkey leg,
While Aunt Sue juggles eggs, what a peg!

Laughter spills like gravy wide,
As Cousin Bob runs to hide.
Mom's brussels sprouts start to roll,
We munch and crunch, out of control!

Sister's trying to keep her face,
From a mouthful—what a race!
Dad's jokes land with loads of cheese,
Thankful hearts, oh, can't you see?

With every bite, a silly tale,
Spontaneous dance, we cannot fail.
Here's to meals that bring us close,
And memories we all love the most!

The Language of Thanks

At our table, words do fly,
As Grandma rolls her pie so high.
Cousins trade their favorite snacks,
While Uncle Larry shows us hacks!

'Thank you' said with mouth so full,
Is quite a sight, and rather dull.
Yet with every bite we chime,
In this odd, but tasty rhyme!

Sister's mashed potatoes high,
Make Dad blink and wonder why.
'Thankful for the chaos here,
And all the love—our hearts sincere!'

In the clatter, smiles abound,
With every giggle, joy is found.
Our tidy meals turn wild and grand,
In this language we understand!

Cherished Moments

Mom's turkey wobbles with delight,
As we ponder if it took flight.
From stuffed to popped, we're quite the sight,
Between each bite, we giggle bright!

Auntie's casserole slightly burned,
But laughter's what we've all learned.
Grandpa's stories come with spice,
As we nod and eat—oh, so nice!

The dog under the table prays,
For spills upon the floor always.
With thanks we share each silly grin,
In cherished moments, we all win!

So raise your glass and let it clink,
For every bite, we share a wink.
Through laughter loud and hearty cheer,
We bless this meal, all gathered near!

Joy in Every Bite

With every forkful, giggles rise,
As we devour the least-wise.
A kale smoothie? Who thought of that?
But lies don't matter—it's where we're at!

Cousin spills juice all on the floor,
Suddenly we all want more!
Laughter echoes, fills the space,
In this chaotic, happy place.

Grandma's cookies, a classic cheer,
Crafted with love, we all hold dear.
But watch out now, the chocolate's gone,
I'd swear it danced right off the dawn!

In every laugh, a joyful bite,
As we indulge 'til the moon sings bright.
Here's to family, food and fun,
In every meal, we're all as one!

Savoring the Moments of Joy

In the kitchen, chaos reigns,
As Auntie trips on her shoelace strains.
The turkey's burnt; the pie's a flop,
Yet laughter rings; we'll never stop.

Uncle Joe sings off-key with pride,
While Grandma nudges, 'Step aside!'
The dog steals a roll, what a sight!
Our hearts are full, but our appetite's light.

Silly stories from days of yore,
As cousin Bob spills punch on the floor.
With every sip, more giggles ensue,
Thankfulness grows for this joyous crew.

As plates pile high with mishaps galore,
We raise our forks; who could want more?
In this banquet of laughter, love, and cheer,
We savor the moments, year after year.

Plates Full of Thanks

Stacks of dishes all piled high,
We welcome each meal with a hopeful sigh.
The salad's too soggy, the bread's gone stale,
But one more round of dessert? We prevail!

With forks in hand and spaghetti fights,
Who knew dinner could reach such heights?
A mountain of mashed it's starting to sway,
Oh, who will be brave and save the day?

The kids are giggling, the dog's at the door,
With pleading eyes, he begs for more.
Chocolate pudding on faces so bright,
Every bite savored, pure delight.

As we count our blessings amidst the great mess,
We share our stories with humor and zest.
Though there's crumbs on the floor, we're all grinning
wide,
Our plates full of thanks, we eat with pride.

Tapestry of Thankfulness

We gather 'round in merry delight,
With mismatched socks; our outfits are tight.
The centerpiece wobbles, it's hung by a thread,
Yet we giggle and munch, no signs of dread.

A laugh from the corner, Dad's telling a joke,
Mom rolls her eyes, 'Here comes the smoke!'
The cat steals the turkey; oh what a mess,
We're grateful for humor, we must confess.

Green beans are flying, watch out for your head!
With each silly moment, we're easily fed.
As stories weave 'round like a warm blanket's wrap,
This tapestry glows, no time for a nap.

So here's to this gathering, a whimsical blast,
With every mishap, good memories cast.
In the fabric of laughter and love we partake,
Thankful for moments, more joyous to make.

The Table of Togetherness

At this table, chaos takes the lead,
With spilled juice and laughter, there's plenty indeed.
Sticky fingers, sweet pies on our face,
Yet everyone's smiling in this crazy place.

Grandpa's snoring, he's lost in his dreams,
While Grandma's planning the next great schemes.
With each clink of glasses and cheerful toast,
We're thankful for family; we love it the most.

The kids are playing a game of charades,
As Uncle Tim's belly becomes the charades.
With hugs and with giggles, our hearts swell with glee,
In this delightful circus, we're all family.

So raise your glass for a toast of delight,
For moments that sparkle like stars in the night.
At this wondrous table, with fond hearts and laughs,
We cherish togetherness, the best of our halves.

The Abundance of Kindness

A turkey flew high, on a whim and a dare,
As mashed potatoes giggled, light as the air.
Gravy started dancing, on the table it spun,
While the carrots were joking, saying, 'Look at us run!'

The cranberry sauce, in a sassy bright hue,
Whispered to peas, 'Hey, do you think we're a stew?'
Potato rolls chuckled, bread baskets in tow,
While the stuffing, now blushing, said, 'Just let me go!'

A toast for the feast, with glasses held high,
The broccoli yelled, 'We're the green, oh me, my!'
With laughter abound, and the hearts feeling light,
Even the candles danced, giving off a warm light.

As laughter erupted, and sweet treats came near,
Pumpkin pies winked, 'We are the stars here!'
Each scoop of ice cream, took a jig in delight,
The table of laughter, oh what a fine sight!

Savoring Sweet Moments

In the kitchen, the cookies were dancing in rows,
Twirling and swirling, like nobody knows.
The brownies were rumbling, 'We're fudgy and fine,'
While cupcakes were sharing a secret design.

With sprinkles that sparkled like stars up above,
Marshmallows whispered, 'Don't we all just love?
The taste of the laughter, the joy that we bring,
Even the cereal packets started to sing.'

Pies lost their crusts, just spooling around,
And the ice cream took note, it was melting, all brown!
'Save me a scoop!' shouted the jelly bean crew,
As each flavor popped out, with a wink and a chew.

Together they laughed, a delightful parade,
Savoring moments, in a long, sweet cascade.
Slurping and munching, what great olden times,
With the cookies telling jokes, sweetened with rhymes!

Hues of Gratitude

In the garden where colors bloom bright as a song,
The carrots are blushing, they feel they belong.
The peas, all in green, are waving with cheer,
While the oranges chuckle, 'Look how we appear!'

The corn sent a message, through kernels galore,
'We're golden and cheerful, we're never a bore!'
Radishes giggled, their tops playfully swayed,
While beets sang in purple, so grandly displayed.

With fruits and fresh veggies having a ball,
Each thankful hue painted the backdrop of all.
'We're vibrant, we're jolly, we're flavors unite,
Reminding each heart of the simple delight!'

As every dish sparkled, in the warm autumn glow,
The hues of appreciation began to show.
With laughter and veggies, this bounty's a hit,
Thankfulness simmering, in every small bit!

A Tapestry of Thanks

A cornucopia crafted with giggles and glee,
Each item on display, as proud as can be.
The legumes were plotting a festive charade,
While the tomatoes blushed, booster shots they made.

The napkins were folding themselves for a dance,
With forks and spoons winking, giving glances askance.
'Let's twirl about!' cried the bright salad bowl,
While the dressing poured out, as if to console.

'Have you met the biscuits? They simply can't miss!
Rolling away, in a buttery bliss!'
The jams started singing, in their jars they proclaimed,
While each note of laughter, the spreaders all claimed.

In this feast of delight, as fun intertwined,
A tapestry woven with joy defined.
Each morsel delightful, each smile a spark,
This banquet of delight, oh, the joy in the dark!

Toasts Under the Stars

We gather round with cheer and glee,
With glasses raised, just you and me.
The punch is spiked, or so we say,
And laughs abound in wild display.

The stars above, they twinkle bright,
As we toast to snacks that feel just right.
A burnt pie here, a charred roast there,
Yet still we feast without a care.

We share our tales of kitchen fails,
Of soup gone wrong, and floppy tails.
Each bite becomes a memory,
With side remarks and jokes set free.

So lift your cup, let laughter flow,
For friends like these, you surely know.
In silly moments, hearts will blend,
To toast to life, and love, and friends.

Bonds of Appreciation

Gather 'round, oh merry crew,
With grateful hearts as we chew.
Our table creaks with endless munch,
Did grandma really bake that lunch?

The salad danced upon my plate,
A wobbly side, it's truly fate.
Old Uncle Joe spills dressing wide,
But laughter's here, we let it slide.

We pass the dishes, share a grin,
With every bite comes ribbing kin.
A toast for every awkward glance,
To joy and pie, let's skip the dance!

Hey, what's that in the casserole?
Is it a dish or a black hole?
Yet here we sit, with hearts so bold,
The laughter warm, the memories gold.

A Symphony of Gratitude

A banquet laid with love and cheer,
But who forgot the drinks, oh dear!
The turkey's singing, or at least it tries,
As grandma's laughter fills the skies.

Oh, the jello jiggles with delight,
While cousins throw their spoons in spite.
The pie takes flight, oh what a sight,
We clap for crumbs that dance in light.

The rhythm's off, but we don't mind,
In this wild mix, true joy we find.
Each silly story brings us near,
A symphony that's loud and clear.

With chopsticks, forks, and funny scripts,
We savor all the wordy quips.
Let's raise a cheer for food and friends,
In this great jest, the laughter never ends.

Heartfelt Gatherings

They come from far with dishes rare,
I bring the rolls, but do they care?
Our hearts are full, our pants are tight,
As we toast to love long into the night.

So grab your plate, don't be so shy,
Just watch out for Aunt Sue's sweet pie.
It's rumble time, the flavors clash,
But who can stop this food-filled bash?

There's buttered bread and chaos too,
Every bite brings giggles anew.
Our hearts convene, a lovely sight,
As we agree, dessert's in sight!

With toasts and jokes and clanging snacks,
In bowls of cheer, we've got no lacks.
Here's to us, the fun and quirks,
In heartfelt gatherings, we're all jerks.

Banquet of Joy

Gather 'round the table, what a sight,
Turkey doing the tango, oh what a delight.
Grandma's famous stuffing stealing the show,
Uncle Joe's dance moves? You've got to see those go!

Creamy mashed potatoes piled way too high,
Sister's brussels sprouts make the dog nearby cry.
Pie fights break out, whipped cream in the air,
And Auntie's lost again, she's in the wrong chair!

Laughter erupts as the stories unfold,
The tales of great Uncle, always bold.
Cousins bump elbows, spill juice on the floor,
Who knew this gathering would start a galore?

Peeking at desserts, the goodies align,
Sweets that will have us thanking divine.
In this banquet of joy, we cherish with glee,
What's better than laughter and love, can't you see?

Cornucopia of Memories

A table piled high with food galore,
Grandpa's old stories, we all implore.
Cousins cracking jokes, oh what a scene,
With gravy on our shirts, we're the in-crowd cuisine!

The dog begs for turkey, he's eyeing the feast,
While the cat's on a mission, from corner to east.
A dash of spilled soda, a sprinkle of cheer,
With mess and mayhem, we're all gathered here.

As pies take their turns on the squeaky old rack,
The pumpkins roll on, there's no looking back.
Ice cream is melting, it dribbles and spills,
But laughter is served, it's our favorite thrill.

With each passing course and overstuffed plate,
These moments remind us of life's best fate.
From mishaps to giggles, our hearts intertwine,
In this cornucopia, the joy is divine!

Heartfelt Offerings

Gather 'round folks, it's that time of year,
When calories don't count, and there's nothing to fear.
The vegetable platter? Just for the show,
As we devour the pie, like it's a rodeo!

Grandma's secret recipe, too spicy to tell,
A dash of embarrassment under the spell.
With plates piled high, we engage in our arts,
Making sauce stains that don't mend our hearts.

The napkins are crumpled, the laughter is bright,
We roast each other—what a glorious sight.
The turkey is brave, taking all in stride,
While the cranberry sauce takes a wild ride!

As we scoop up the dessert, smiles in our eyes,
Reflections of friends, like pie in the skies.
With each heartfelt offering, we know it's true,
The irony's sweet; it's a love we all brew.

The Spirit of Togetherness

With table stretched wide, friendships ignite,
A food fight erupts, what a hilarious sight!
Someone calls "Fire!" as the oven door pops,
But we savor together, till the last drop stops.

The spirit's alive in the chaos we cook,
Dad's dancing like a turkey, just take a look!
The kids try to hide their smirks behind pies,
While we burst into laughter, oh how time flies.

From sweet potatoes singing with sugar and fun,
To pudding that wiggles, it's all just begun.
With seconds and thirds, we embrace the delight,
Who knew togetherness could taste so right?

So here's to the moments when laughter is shared,
In the warmth of these faces, we know we have cared.
For every heart joined, in this festive parade,
The spirit of togetherness—our love's true crusade!

Sunlight on Our Plates

Sunshine spills on bowls of stew,
While Auntie spills her drink anew.
Mashed potatoes dance on the side,
The turkey's gone, oh where'd it hide?

Grandpa's snoring, what a delight,
While cousins bicker, ready for a bite.
The pie looks round, but tastes like flair,
Who knew those carrots gave such a scare?

Uncle's jokes are cheesy and warm,
Yet, strangely, nothing can de-form.
Laughter echoes, fills the air,
Thanksgiving chaos, we all share.

So raise your glass, don't spill that fizz,
We'll toast to food, and family biz!
With every bite, there's joy unrolled,
Thankful hearts, in laughter bold.

Seeds of Thankfulness

We plant our love with creamy dips,
As dad serves up those tasty chips.
The salad's green, oh but beware,
A hidden beet? Oh, that's unfair!

With each bite, we giggle and sigh,
A turkey-shaped cake catches the eye.
Aunt Mae's secret, what could it be?
More sprinkles than the recipe!

Grandpa's stories come thick like stew,
But we all know they're mostly untrue.
We roll our eyes and stifle a snort,
As laughter sprouts, a comical sport.

So let's raise our forks and dig in deep,
With seeds of joy that we will keep.
Grinning faces, tales that swell,
In this happy chaos, all is swell.

The Colors of Thanksgiving

Colors burst from the dinner spread,
Pumpkin orange and cranberry red.
But what's that green? Is it for real?
Or just a plan to make us squeal?

Potatoes mountains, fluffy and white,
They tower tall, a most glorious sight.
Watch out for gravy, it's on a roll,
A slippery path to the dinner bowl.

Cousins collide in a food parade,
As dessert time hits, all plans are made.
With pie in hand, the battle's begun,
Who'll have the last slice, oh what fun!

So gather round, don the napkin hats,
With every laugh, we just sit like cats.
Colors bright and hearts so light,
Thankful moments, a joyous sight.

Aroma of Togetherness

The scent of goodies wafts through the door,
Grandma's cookies on the kitchen floor.
Her secret recipe lost in a haze,
But boy, the smell puts us in a daze!

We gather near the table high,
Where family stories zoom and fly.
Uncle finds the turkey's funny bone,
Moment captured, Instagram's own!

The stuffing's wild, it tries to flee,
A side-eye glance, "Who cooked this, me?"
A wink, a laugh, the fun continues,
Togetherness blooms, like wild petunias.

So lift your glass, with giggles bright,
For messy meals and shared delight.
In laughter wrapped, love finds its way,
Our grateful hearts in silly play.

Table of Abundance

Plates piled high with food galore,
The turkey's dancing, who could ask for more?
Mashed potatoes doing the jig,
While grandma's pie just won a gig.

Salads whisper secrets on the side,
The rolls are plotting how to hide!
Cranberries jiggling like they've got a plan,
While Uncle Joe cooks up his giant prawn.

Kids are giggling, making a mess,
Spaghetti threads in a tangled dress.
Fingers sticky, faces bright,
As laughter echoes through the night.

Cheers erupt for every dish,
As Auntie Sue makes her crazy wish.
A toast to all, and let's partake,
In this wild feast, for fun's own sake!

A Celebration of Hearts

Gather 'round, let's sing a tune,
The cat's on the table, plotting doom!
With pie on his head and cream in his paw,
Who knew our dinner had a furry flaw?

Jugs of juice spill like our fate,
As Cousin Tim tries to stand straight.
In the chaos, we find delight,
With laughter echoing through the night.

Grandpa's jokes are older than time,
He cracks one now, oh, that's sublime!
Laughter bubbles, fills the air,
With goofy hats, who could despair?

As we cheer for another round,
Carrots disappear without a sound.
In this circus of love and art,
We celebrate, with messy hearts!

Shared Memories, Shared Meals

What's cooking, friends? Oh, just a show,
Grandma's quirks are in full flow!
She's jigging while stirring, what a sight,
With her apron spinning, oh what delight!

Pasta flings across the room,
As we dodge meatballs like impending doom.
The soup's too hot, we cheer and pout,
But laughter's the soup we can't live without.

The sweet corn pops like fireworks,
While Auntie Sue finds her new quirks.
"More potatoes!" shouts Cousin Lou,
As he juggles three, "Look! I'm a chef too!"

Memories made over every bite,
Lessons learned in the warmth of light.
With every laugh, and slip and slide,
Our happiness is fed from inside.

Grateful Hearts United

With forks held high, we unite with cheer,
As the dog eyes the feast, drawing near.
He's plotting theft, we know the score,
But laughter will save him, if only once more.

Pumpkin pie? Oh, what a thrill!
As my brother tries to eat his fill.
He's got whipped cream all over his face,
But really, who can blame him in this race?

We toast with cups of fizzy drinks,
Sharing thoughts while the food winks.
With every bite, our hearts expand,
In this goofy, merry little band.

So here's to fun, and food galore,
With stories and laughter, who could ask for more?
We gather close, we laugh and we share,
For grateful hearts find humor everywhere.

Heartfelt Delights

With mashed potatoes piled so high,
I fear they'll reach the sky!
Gravy rivers run and flow,
Watch out for the turkey show!

A pie so large, it takes a crew,
To lift it to our view.
We'll dance around the table's edge,
And sign a food-lover's pledge!

Uncle Bob cracks jokes galore,
While Aunt Sue snags one more score.
The cranberry sauce, a gooey friend,
On biscuits, it can happily blend!

Each laugh rings out, a joyful spark,
As we gather, it's a lark.
With plates piled high and hearts so light,
Our silly feast is pure delight!

Embracing the Bounty

Oh, turkey struts, so proud, so wide,
Can there be enough to hide?
Stuffing peeks from every crack,
Just hope there's room for a snack!

A salad bowl that's built like a wall,
Challenging us to eat it all.
The rolls roll past, like bowling balls,
Will they help or cause some falls?

Pumpkin spice in every drink,
We sip and giggle, start to think.
'Is there pie?' the children scream,
As we float through this food-filled dream!

With bellies full, we take a break,
A dance-off to a food coma shake.
Laughter echoes, joy will stay,
As we munch our hearts away!

A Symphony of Sincere Thanks

With forks that clatter and plates that dance,
We all join in a foodie trance.
A chorus of cheers, a bubbling stew,
Is it time for seconds? Yep, I think so too!

A gravy boat sails across the floor,
Filling our plates and asking for more.
The mashed potatoes stand so brave,
Next to the beans, they start to wave!

Napkins tossed, the fun begins,
As cousins compete for the biggest wins.
Desserts parade, a sugar ballet,
With crumbs and giggles on display!

Thankful hearts in every bite,
As we savor each delight.
So pass the food, make merry sounds,
In this silly dance where joy abounds!

The Warmth of Shared Blessings

Gather 'round the crowded table,
A feast that's truly quite unstable!
Spilled drinks and laughter fill the air,
We all look up and everyone stares!

The green beans giggle, the corn does waltz,
As we dish out helpings without any faults.
Grandad starts to sing a tune,
While Grandma shushes by the spoon!

In this chaos, joy is found,
With every clink and every sound.
The pie's on fire, or so it seems,
"Just kidding!" I laugh, "This isn't dreams!"

With every bite, a warm embrace,
We share in joy, in love, in space.
For every smile and silly grin,
We celebrate where all began!

Melodies of Appreciation

In the kitchen, pots do clink,
While grandma brews her special drink.
The turkey's dancing on the shelf,
While the dog is eyeing it with stealth.

Cousins argue over who can eat,
As the pies are rolling in the heat.
We raise a toast with soda pop,
Then hear dad's belly rumble, flop!

Grandpa's stories never get old,
About the time he danced with bold.
A fun-filled day, of laughter keen,
With pie stains forming quite a scene!

So gather 'round with cheer and glee,
For hearty meals, and love with glee.
With every laugh, we fill our part,
In this joyful gathering of the heart!

Celebrating with Open Hearts

The table's set with plates galore,
Dishes stacked, can't hold them more.
A salad tucked behind the roast,
Who's here to judge? We're here to boast!

Mom's overcooked the green bean dish,
While Uncle Bob dreams of a wish.
He wishes turkey came in a vat,
With extra gravy, how about that?

Sister spills her drink with flair,
While laughs erupt like autumn air.
We eat and giggle, bolts of fun,
As dad snores softly, he's just begun!

The pie parade approaches fast,
Chop, chop, chop, the slices cast.
We'll be talking for years to come,
About the day when fun was hum!

Recipes of Remembrance

A recipe book, so tattered and worn,
Yet every page, new flavors are born.
We stir the memories just like stew,
With a dash of laughter and happiness too!

A pinch of this and a sprinkle there,
Grandma's secrets whispered with flair.
The bread's too doughy, but who will care?
It tastes like love, served warm with air.

The pie's an epic, the crust all thick,
Sister's gone rogue with a baking trick.
While cousins try to snag a slice,
With eyes so wide, not once but thrice!

These gatherings mix both spice and cheer,
With each recommendation we hold dear.
So raise a spoon, let laughter start,
As we savor the taste of every heart!

Nourishment of the Spirit

Gathered 'round, the chairs are tight,
With servings matching appetites.
The cranberry sauce, a jelly glow,
Mom swears it's the best, you know!

Uncle's telling tales from days of yore,
We're laughing so hard, we ask for more.
His pants get tighter with every bite,
Oh, how we'll joke into the night!

The macaroni fights with the peas,
In a bowl of chaos, if you please.
Sister's in charge of crafty decor,
With ribbons stuck and glitter galore!

So here we sit, a merry band,
With every scoop, we're hand in hand.
In glorious love, the meal's just fine,
With hearts so full, we're feeling divine!

Harvest of Gratitude

In the kitchen, chaos reigns,
A turkey does the cha-cha with the grains.
Potatoes roll and dance away,
As we laugh at all the mischief today.

Pumpkin pie is on the rise,
Wobbling like a prize surprise.
Everyone's trying to steal a taste,
But here comes the dog, oh what a waste!

Cranberry sauce in a gooey line,
Some say it's just divine.
But Frank from next door dips a chip,
And asks us if this could be a trip!

So here we are with all this cheer,
Wishing every laugh is sincere.
With food and friends, we won't complain,
Let's eat and giggle till it rains again!

Banquet of Blessings

Table's set with flair and zest,
Who knew cooking could be a test?
Grandma's recipe calls for a dash,
But she's been known for a mischievous splash.

Kids are juggling bread rolls high,
While Aunt May laughs, oh me, oh my!
Salt's mistaken for the sugar jar,
This sweet potato pie is quite bizarre!

Sipping cider that tastes like clover,
Laughing so hard, we roll right over.
The chicken's awkwardly in a twist,
But no one dares to make a list.

So gather 'round with joy and fun,
With each dish, we've surely won.
In this banquet, love's the host,
And laughter's what we love the most!

The Abundance of Appreciation

Dinner's served, what a sight!
But somehow the soup's turned bright.
Everyone claims it's 'avant-garde',
While Uncle Joe thinks it's a jarred card.

A cornucopia of flavors bold,
Laughter shines brighter than gold.
Mismatched silverware tells the tale,
Of a gathering where we'll never fail.

The bread rolls bounce like tiny balls,
As we reminisce about the falls.
A mishap here, a giggle there,
Who knew cooking could lead to despair?

So count your blessings, toast in glee,
With laughter echoing, wild and free.
In this feast of mishaps and delights,
Every cringeworthy bite ignites our nights!

Gathering of Grateful Souls

Here we gather, plates piled high,
With turkey legs that make us sigh.
But here comes Cousin Fred with a grin,
Stumbling over his own shoelace thin.

The salad bowl spins like a top,
Tomatoes fly and then they plop.
"Do you really think fresh is best?"
"I don't know, but pass the jest!"

Gravy's splattered on a bright chair,
Everyone's laughing without a care.
A toast for the things that went awry,
With every slip-up, we're flying high.

So raise your glass, let the giggles roll,
In this gathering, we feel the whole.
For in every moment that we share,
Gratitude's found everywhere!

Seasons of Giving

In spring, we bring salad with glee,
But summer's for picnics, just you wait and see.
Fall's all about pumpkins, quite the sight,
While winter's for cocoa, and marshmallows light.

We laugh as we nibble on leftovers galore,
With family around, who could want more?
Each season a reason for joy and delight,
Like a pie in the face — oh what a fright!

So toast to the seasons and quirky tastes,
With spoonfuls of laughter, there's seldom a waste.
Let's cherish these moments, hair-raising and bold,
As we feast on the memories, and stories retold.

In this gathering of souls, we can't help but cheer,
With pie that's been burned — we'll still persevere!
For love is the secret, the spice that we add,
To this spectacular banquet, of funny and mad.

Shared Plates

At the table, we gather, what a sight to behold,
With plates overflowing, and stories retold.
You take my fries, and I'll steal your cake,
With each little nibble, our laughter will wake.

The mashed potatoes fight back like a champ,
As awkwardness lingers like an old-fashioned lamp.
We giggle and gasp, with mouths full of food,
Sharing our secrets — both silly and crude.

From leftover turkey that smells like a shoe,
To epic desserts that we dare to pursue.
Each bite is a treasure, each sip a delight,
In this joyous adventure, we share with delight.

When the dessert comes, oh what a parade,
A sugar rush party, nobody's afraid.
With plates all together, we bring on the cheers,
In the end, it's our laughter that truly endears.

Full Hearts

With bellies all full, we share giddy grins,
As crumbs scatter wildly, like mischievous sins.
Who knew that a taco could be such a treat?
Yet somehow it's just what unites all we eat.

Spilling sweet tea and making a splash,
Oh, what a picture — a wobbly bash!
Our hearts full of giggles, our plates piled high,
As we trade silly faces — oh my, oh my!

As we lose our tempers, and forks go astray,
Cheesecake diplomacy lights up the day.
Though pie may go splat, we hold hands with cheer,
For love is the reason we all gather here.

Let's raise a toast to this lovable mess,
With laughter and lifting glasses, we feel so blessed.
It's in being a family that really feels right,
From the silliest moments, to each warm bite.

Embracing the Gifts of Life

Life's little gifts come wrapped up with flair,
A casserole that wobbles, a pie in the air.
With each quirky dish, and odd little seat,
We savor the chaos as wild as a feat.

Who knew that a salad could bring so much fun?
With dressing that dances like a bright little sun.
From friendship that simmers to laughter so light,
Here's to the moments that sparkle so bright!

We toast to the mischief, grand tales that we tell,
Like tripping on cupcakes or spilling a gel.
Each flop a reminder, each slip a delight,
For life's a grand feast when we let it ignite.

So let's fill our plates with whatever we find,
From noodles so tangled, to desserts unrefined.
With laughter as seasoning, we dig in with pride,
For every mishap is better side by side.

A Mosaic of Thankful Souls

In a world full of flavors that mingle with cheer,
We gather like colors, so vibrant and dear.
With laughter as glue and stories so bold,
Each soul adds a hue to the memories retold.

Oh, the pasta disasters that squiggled and fell,
Missing spoons increase the air of our swell.
Yet as we all giggle through the ups and the downs,
We find joy in the mess and wear silly crowns.

Like veggies in salad, we all play a part,
Stirring up laughter, it's an art from the heart.
With plates piled high, and smiles ear to ear,
We hold to each other like treasures held dear.

For a mosaic of souls is a canvas of fun,
Where love's only ingredient is never outdone.
So here's to the gathering, the quirks that arise,
A blend of affection, that sparkles and flies.

Milton Keynes UK
Ingram Content Group UK Ltd.
UKHW021915201124
451474UK00013B/756

9 789916 943618